Published in Western Australia
by Sandpiper Press
2 Prowse Street, West Perth, W.A. 6005

First published 1989

National Library of Australia
Cataloguing-in-publication data
Woldendorp, Richard Leo, 1927
Sandpiper Press
ISBN 0 9596934-2-4

Printed in Singapore by Tien Wah Press (Pte.) Ltd

Typeset in Western Australia
by Image Communications, West Perth.

Film processing by Churchill
Colour Laboratories

Western Australia

VIEW WEST

Richard Woldendorp

AUTHOR'S NOTE

'View West' is my attempt to give a broad picture of Western Australia – of its landscapes, its industries and its people. It is an up-dating of my previous books 'Looking West' and 'Australia's West', for the state is developing at such a rate that, from time to time, a review of this kind seems necessary.

It is always a challenge for me to try to depict, with so few pictures, such an enormously large area and such a range of possibilities. I trust that what I have chosen is representational of the land the people who live here.

I would like to thank the many individuals and the companies who have always given me such generous assistance in my obtaining of photographs. And I am most appreciative of the steady support of my wife Lyn who has helped me in so many ways. Together, we have all made this project possible.

Ansett
Argyle Diamond Sales Limited
Baillieu Knight Frank (W.A.) Pty Ltd
Barrington Partners
Baxter Marketing
Burswood Resort Casino
Government of Western Australia
Hamersley Iron Pty Ltd
Houghton Wines Pty Ltd
Marine Industries Ltd
Monkey Mia Dolphin Resort
Quality Pacific Hotels Limited
The Rural and Industries Bank of Western Australia
Slingair Pty Ltd
Wesfarmers Limited
Western Mining Corporation Limited
Woodside Offshore Petroleum Pty Ltd
Worsley Alumina Pty Ltd

You can stand beside Richard Woldendorp with exactly the same camera in your hand, use the same film, the same setting, frame the same subject exactly, yet he'll produce a startlingly original image – and you'll finish up with a snap.

The difference is, quite simply, that he sees things the rest of us don't.

Call it the artist's eye, if you will.

No one who has ever seen his photographs could be the least bit surprised to know that, as a young man in Holland, Richard trained in fine arts.

Every shot he takes demonstrates his innate, visual sensitivity.

(His private collection of his own youthful paintings are rich with serious artistic promise.)

As it fell out, photography became his medium and, since his ambitious canvas is no less than Australia itself, we can be glad he chose the camera rather than the brush.

As a painter he might have given us a few dozen images.

The speed and flexibility of photography has enabled him to capture the visual essence of our lovely country in a thousand original ways.

Richard's European sensibility has worked for him, and us. Just as Joseph Conrad reinvented the English language by coming at it from a radically different angle so, too, does Richard re-interpret Australia, coming at it with breathtaking obliqueness.

Lately for instance, like some benign deity, he has been hovering above the continent in planes and helicopters, revealing to us the ancient, time-sculptured bones, skin and sinews of our Great South Land. By ascending heavenwards he has unlocked for himself, and us, a veritable Lassiter's Reef of new images, astonishing in their subtlety and beauty. Triumphantly, he has solved the visual problem of our limiting 'horizonability' with a unique and sustained insight.

It is this lateral approach – the mark of a formidable intellect – that sets this world apart.

I've had the pleasure of watching him develop as an artist for a quarter of a century.

As this new collection of images bears witness, his talent continues to burgeon in a sweet, exponential curve.

Bill Warnock. *June, 1989.*

Perth is beautifully sited on the Swan, just where the river broadens out into wide stretches of water. This gives the feeling of space within the city itself. And there are high points – Kings' Park is one – which allow sweeping views beyond the city and the river to the backdrop of the Darling Ranges. The eye is not barricaded in by buildings as in many other cities. I live in the bush, in those hills, commuting regularly to Perth, and as I cross the river each day I delight in the many moods of its great expanse of water – ever-changing and always a pleasure to the photographer's eye.

I find the metropolitan area to be still of a comfortable size, with reasonably quick access to most places (a "twenty minute city" someone once called it). However, it is growing, and this feeling of comfort may well be lost if the low-density suburban sprawl continues. I, for one, would like to see more use made of the waterway which is central to this growth, more restaurants, cafes, tearooms, where people can sit and enjoy the things this remarkable place has to offer.

The Perth way of life is a relaxed one. Fine beaches lie all along the coast from Two Rocks to Mandurah. Rottnest, an island as naturally beautiful as any Greek island, is only an hour away by boat. New beach and resort developments at Two Rocks and Yanchep in the north balance those already in the south around Mandurah. Favoured as it is by ocean and river, it is no wonder that Perth attracts people to water-sports – surfing, swimming, sailing, water skiing; for the ease of access to the water is complemented by the climate – eight hours a day average sunshine.

Fremantle is a separate city, twenty kilometres from Perth yet merging with it. Its character is distinct, for it has been willing to conserve its past – its historical monuments as a port, and its beautiful old houses and hotels. High-rise development, which so often alienates people, has no place here. I always enjoy visiting Fremantle, for the scale and the style of its buildings is human; and unlike Perth, it has used its waterways well. It is a place that invites people to come together, attracting many from the outer suburbs to its markets, its restaurants and its fishing harbour.

Northbridge, north of Perth, attracts people too. It is a centre of multi-culturalism where it is possible to savour the food and hear the language of almost every Asian and European country, for a steady influx of people from other lands has greatly enriched our society. As a comparative newcomer from Holland I greatly appreciate this aspect of the city.

Despite its claim to be the most isolated capital in the world, Perth is large enough to have overseas recognition and to draw visits from international celebrities. The Festival of Perth is the annual focus of these visits, and the West Australian Art Gallery exhibits regularly the works of famous artists. Isolated perhaps, but certainly not out of touch.

At the same time this isolation has led to a strong sense of identity in the West Australian, who is proud of his state and his origins. Nerve centre of the largest state in Australia, Perth services an area of over 1.6 million square kilometres, a great space where the population is thinly-spread. West Australians, like other Australians, tend to cluster on the edges of their continent, where the water is. For beyond lies the harshness and the dryness of the interior.

Jetty at South Perth. Reflections of the city on a balmy summer's evening.

The impressively renovated Palace Hotel at the corner of St George's Terrace and William Street. Now a banking chamber.

The classic view of Perth from King's Park.

Recently landscaped park at South Perth.

*From Mounts Bay Road –
a landscaped garden where
the river once ran.*

A mosaic of high-rise.

'Downtown' Perth City.
Beautifully sited on the Swan River.

Sailing on the Swan River.

People of all ages at the start of
the Bridge-to-Bridge marathon.

15.

Moorings at Royal Perth Yacht Club.

Any summer weekend at Crawley.

Fast food outlet – part of the city scene.

Carillon Arcade, Perth.

Hay Street – the main shopping precinct – looking west.

Stately facade of the old Post Office from the new Forrest Chase shopping complex.

21.

Central Perth – a place to sit.

Forecourt – Art Gallery of Western Australia.

The old, seen from the new – Perth Technical College from Alexander Library.

Winthrop Hall – University of Western Australia – Crawley.

Government House, Swan River, Narrows Bridge and Kings Park providing the backdrop.

West Australian Ballet Company rehearsal.

Festival of Perth concert at the Quarry Amphitheatre, Reabold Hill.

Street theatre, Northbridge.

Circus Oz at the Burswood Convention Centre showroom.

Contemporary sculpture gallery, Middle Swan.

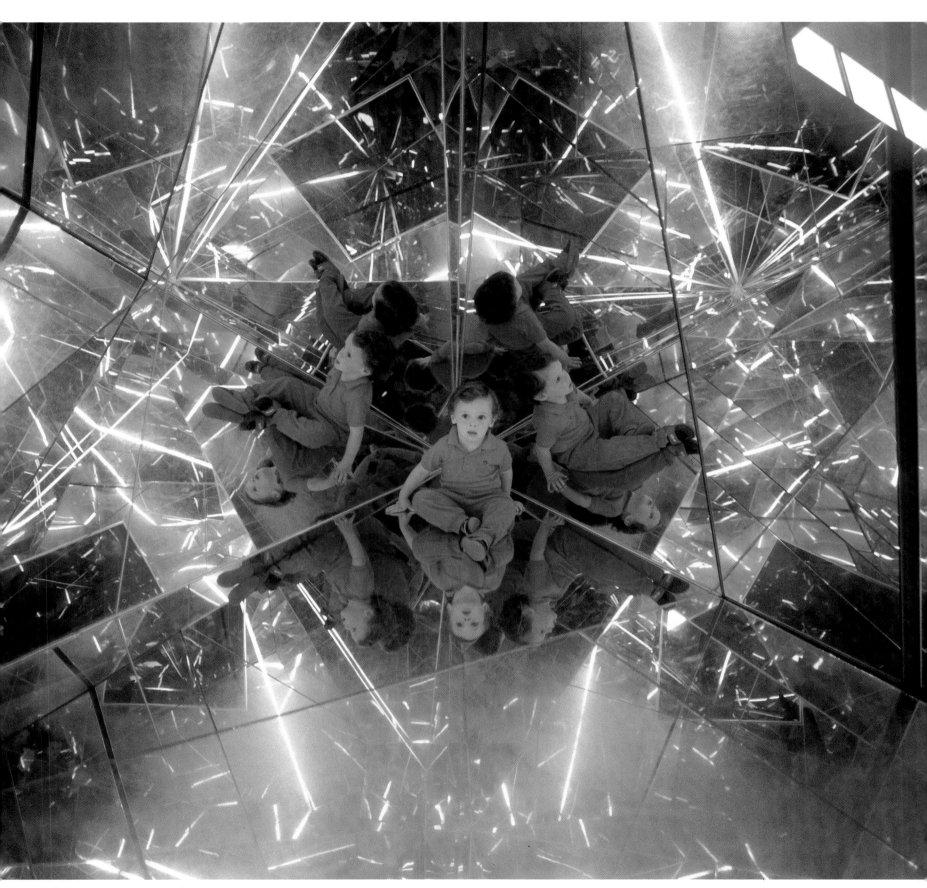

Sci-Tech – Discovery centre at City West.

Northbridge – a multi-cultural meeting place.

City busker.

High-flier Leon Pericles – maker of kites.

Joan Campbell, Potter.

Golf course, part of the Burswood Hotel complex.

*The marina at Hillarys,
one of the new waterfront
developments north of Perth.*

Underwater World at Hillarys.

Aerial view of Yanchep marina and the Atlantis Marine Park.

Old Mill at South Perth with trappings of the past.

Pub in South Perth, a popular drinking place, typical of the fashionable revival of the old pub style.

Visual pollution, a result of our materialistic values, is to be found in all Australian cities.

King's Park, a large area of
bushland in the heart of the city.

Putting things into place. One of the city car parks near the Perth Concert Hall.

Parking facilities at the Fremantle Sailing Club.

The suburban dream in brick and tile.

*Fremantle from the air.
The river winds its way from
Perth, seen in the background.*

The outdoor charm of Fremantle on a summer's day. Much of the city was re-built and refurbished for the America's Cup.

Old building converted to an art gallery, High Street, Fremantle.

A waterfront seafood restaurant on Fishing Boat Harbour, one of the buildings that sprang up at the time of the America's Cup.

Fishing for chips, Fremantle.

The windy coast is ideal for the popular sport of wind-surfing.

Aerial view of a surf carnival at Cottesloe.

The joy of winning.

Not war paint but the great Australian sun barrier – coloured zinc cream.

Junior surf life-saving carnival at Mullaloo.

Room for everyone.

Lovely beaches – lovely girls.

55

Live sheep transport to the Middle East. Moslem tradition demands this form of meat export.

Perth Airport.

Wheat for the world – loading grain at the Cooperative Bulk Handling Terminal, Kwinana.

Aerial view of Kwinana on Cockburn Sound, centre of heavy industries.

Farming flowers, Spearwood.

Sampling the vintage.

The work force is multi-cultural.

Houghton's winery in the Swan Valley.
This has been a renowned wine-growing
area since the early days of settlement.

Football – where the Eagles dare.

Country cricket.

Taking a break between events at the Brigadoon Equestrian Centre.

*Basketball at the Superdrome.
The Wildcats in action.*

A new river resort development on the Murray, between Ravenswood and Mandurah.

The food-rich environment of Mandurah Estuary attracts many birds.

Early morning – John Forrest National Park in the Darling Ranges, east of Perth.

Because of its much higher rainfall, the Kimberleys have an aspect quite different from that of the Pilbara. The land is not so naked. There is spinifex still, but more grassland, particularly near the coast, and there are certainly more trees.

The coast is fascinating. Eight to ten metre tides have sculptured and indented the shoreline. Seen from the air, the crazy mud flats of Derby look like trees, or like big fingers outspread and daily at work as the tide draws different pictures – changes of form and colour that are faster and more fluid than those of a stony landscape. The mangroves skirting the creeks are best appreciated from the air. It can be dangerous to get into them by boat – and one's sense of timing needs to be exact because of the tidal rise and fall.

Derby is the gateway to the rugged South Kimberley landscape with its mountains and gorges. To visit Broome is something different. Fine beaches, clear waters and a romantic past in the pearling industry, which has resulted in a colourful multicultural population – all these things draw the tourists.

Water is not the precious commodity that it is in the Pilbara. Lake Argyle is full of it, so is the Ord River which supports a great tropical market garden, producing bananas, mangoes, peanuts and other crops. And when the cyclones roar down, the Ord and the Fitzroy can turn into mighty waterways, sweeping all before them.

I have been down the Sale and Hunter rivers and seen the remnants of tropical rain forest along their banks. I have flown over the Oscar, the Durack and The Ragged Ranges and marvelled at the strength of their shapes and the variety of their rocky make-up –

soft sandstone to hardened limestone to granite. But the Bungle Bungles are probably the most intriguing of these weird land forms.

Once I walked down Piccaninny Gorge there, following the river to its head. It was a beautiful shaded walk. And I experienced that feeling often felt in the Kimberleys – a sense of discovery, of being the first to tread that way. I am moved by the freedom and the generosity of this largely untouched landscape and it is an appreciation heightened by an awareness of its fragility. With this feeling there comes also appreciation for the Aboriginal who could survive here for thousands of years and could possibly have continued to do so for thousands more. Can we do the same? We do not have to depend on their skills to do so but it would be an asset for us to understand their mode of survival. Their treatment of the land was gentle; they personalised it and they respected it.

So did many of the early comers who with stamina and perseverance carved some fine cattle stations from the wilderness. But later abuse of the land, due to the temptation of over-grazing has, along with the ravages of donkeys, led to the degeneration of some areas. A new social consciousness of the attractions of the beauties of this last frontier of nature leads me to the hope that people and goverment alike will co-operate to preserve it for our enjoyment and for that of future generations.

View of the northern approach to the Bungle Bungles.

Geekie Gorge on the Fitzroy River.

Tidal mud-flat designs at Derby, seen from the air.

Winjama Gorge on the Lennard River, Napier Range.

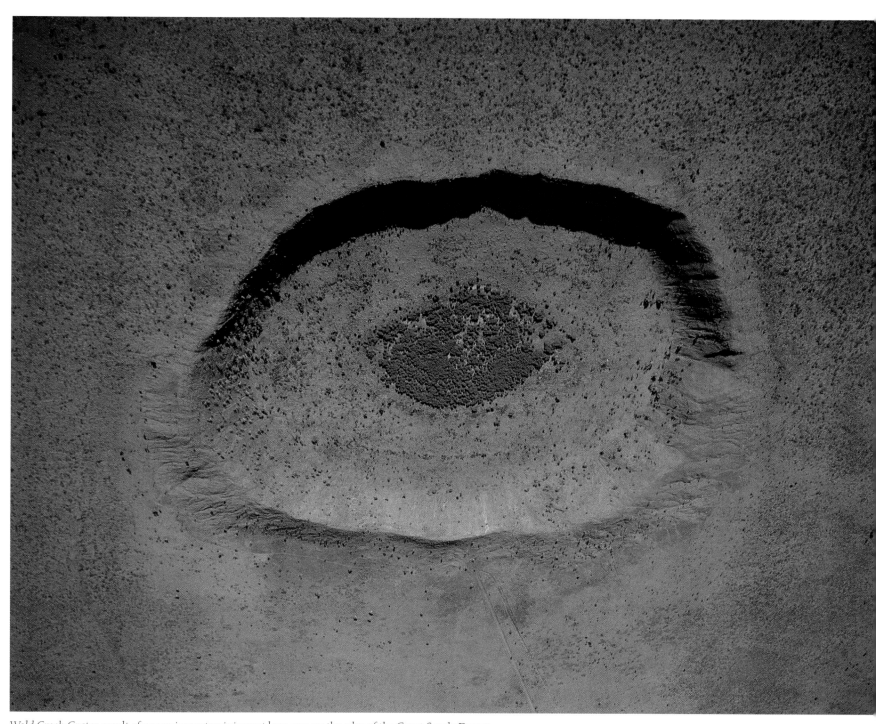

Wold Creek Crater, result of a massive meteoric impact long ago, on the edge of the Great Sandy Desert.

King George River waterfalls.

The rhythm of a Kimberley landscape early morning.

Piccaninny Gorge in the Bungle Bungles.

Cattle mustering on the West Australian/Northern Territory border, Nicholson Station.

Mustering by helicopter in the Kimberleys.

Stockmen of the Kimberleys.

Stockmen's camp.

Jeweller crafting one of Argyle Diamond's pink stones.

Argyle Diamond Mine.

Lake Argyle – large inland body of fresh water.

Ord River overflow near Elephant Rock.

Overleaf:
Town of Kununurra, Kelly's Knob
in the left foreground.

Tourists at magnificent Manning Gorge.

Cable Beach Resort, Broome.

*Sam Lovell, well-known tour leader in the Kimberleys,
pouring a cuppa.*

Bananas grown by irrigation on the Ord River.

Man and camel. Cable Beach.

Camel riding, Cable Beach.

Freshwater crocodiles at the Crocodile Park, Broome.

Children of all races play together on the beach at Broome.

Architecture, Broome style.

Cable Beach. (Top) A monsoonal sky at sunset. (Below) A stroll along the wide stretches.

I have been fascinated by the Pilbara for more than twenty-five years – ever since I went there to photograph the beginning of the iron ore development at Mt Tom Price. I first saw it from the air and I was struck by the strength of its eroded landscape. It is country with its skin showing – for vegetation is sparse, with only the yellow sprinkling of spinifex and the occasional stabbing of a white gum to off-set the rough red of its rocks. Unlike younger ranges with their folds and up thrusts, this is a landscape of subtraction. It is the wearing away of what once was over millions of years that reminds me of the enormous antiquity of this place.

I looked out from the plane to an image of starkness. Broad rivers, empty of water knit the land together in strange patterns (although this dryness is somewhat relieved by rock pools, welcome watering places that sustain life for the animals, and for the humans who venture there; and the ghost gums that line the banks of these courses give promise of an underground water supply that never quite dries up). I was further aware of the power of natural erosion in the fragmented red rock faces. Boulders have been broken off and thrown down the slopes, or are lumped together in their bareness. And the tableland is knifed by gorges – deep narrow cuts in the ground that harbour pools and stormy shapes, sculptured by wind and water.

It is hard country – an iron land, you could say – and iron ore is what has brought the big mining companies. They drag the metal out of the ground in large-scale operations that are barely noticeable in the huge environment they happen in.

Moving to the coast is to find Eighty Mile Beach, a colossal stretch of sand supporting vast colonies of sea birds. At Exmouth there are rich prawning grounds; and the coral reef to the west of Rough Range is the most spectacular on the coast.

I see great beauty in the landscape which sweeps away from the sea inland to the Hamersleys and Mt Bruce till it loses itself in the Great Sandy Desert beyond Marble Bar. Stations are there but they are far between. Pioneers came to graze sheep in the early days – now they have turned to cattle, but the growing of both meat and wool is under harsh conditions. The recent gas and iron ore developments have prised the country open further. Largely due to their activities, access has now been given to those who want to experience the beauty of the Hamersleys.

The winter climate is ideal, with warm sunny days that invite activity, though the nights can be extremely cold in the eastern parts, when the wind whips in from the desert. Summer is scalding. Then the tourists stay home, leaving the country to the hardy – the station folk, the miners – and the occasional photographer!

Pannawonica Hill – spinifex-clad rise topped with solid rock.

Oakover River, a permanent pool.

Giant paper-bark trees along the Oakover River on the edge of the Great Sandy Desert.

Spinifex covered hills, Mt Herbert.

Gold spinifex, brown rock.
Typical landscape of the
Burrup Peninsula.

Looking along Dale's Gorge.

Rough Range Gorge, Exmouth.

Last light striking a rock outcrop.

Water-washed cavern of Hancock Gorge.

Aboriginal carvings, Burrup Peninsula.

View from Mt Herbert in the Chichester Range, looking towards Mt Pyramid.

Overleaf: Mt Newman –
a huge iron ore deposit.

Geologist taking samples from drill holes.

*Priming blasting holes at the
iron ore deposit, Mt Tom Price.*

Loading iron ore at Port Hedland.

*Dampier salt, Hamersley iron
ore and Woodside gas plant, all
in line at King's Bay.*

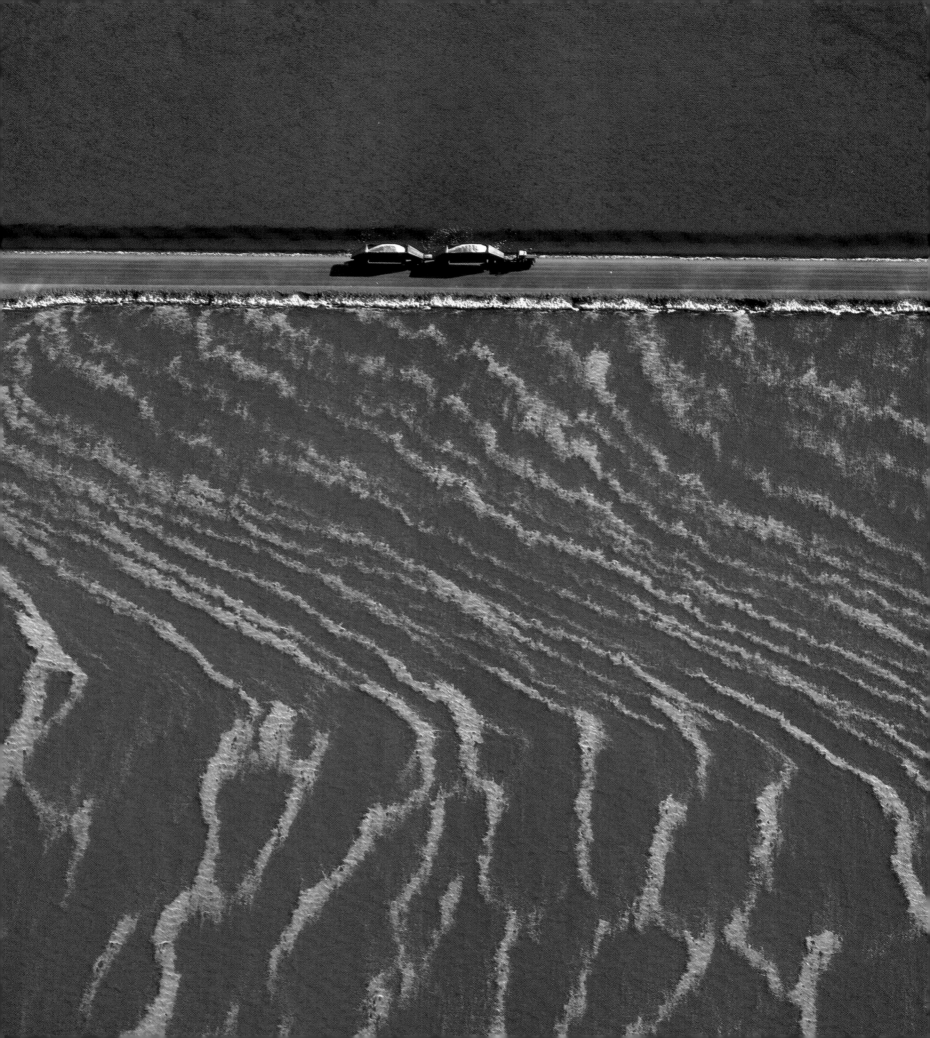

Woodside's L.N.G. (Liquefied Natural Gas) plant at Burrup Peninsula, near Karratha. The plant receives the gas from an off-shore platform.
It pipes some to Perth as natural gas and converts the rest into liquid for export.

The plant at night.

Salt trucks crossing the causeway
through the evaporation ponds.

The human face of industry.

Workers at Woodside.

He who tends the flocks.

Aerial view of A Pilbara sheep station showing the old shearing shed and yards.

Flowers of the region.

Heron on mud flats – Port Hedland.

Birds in flight – Eighty Mile Beach.

This is the area north of Perth, from Carnarvon on the coast inland as far as Meekatharra and Paynes Find, so touching on the goldfields and including parts of the wheat belt. One of the great appeals of this region is the climate which is sunny and stable, milder than Perth in winter and generally more predictable.

The Gascoyne, a large river to the north, ploughs its way through Carnarvon where its waters are tapped for the growing of many crops, such as bananas and tomatoes. I remember the old whaling station there; to me Carnarvon always seemed the last frontier town before going into the Big Country.

I particularly like Shark Bay where a tuck in the coastline provides a tranquil body of water, the first calm seas north of Perth. The western coastline is a legend for its hazard and has devoured many a ship in the past. So it is a relief to come upon these serene waters and to go boating without being smashed to smithereens! In Hamelin Pool the tranquility has made possible some unique developments. Stromatolites, life forms more than three hundred million years old, continue to grow, protected by a salinity too great for most other organisms. They mass together in huge striking clumps. Sea grass grows in the Bay, pasture for those primeval mermaids, the dugong.

At Monkey Mia dolphins and people can get to know one another; and the protective shelter has allowed the build-up of huge bands of shells, deposits up to seventy kilometres long.

Kalbarri at the mouth of the Murchison River, together with its adjacent National Park, attracts many visitors. We once paddled a canoe down the river around the loop and it is the best way to appreciate the beauty of the gorge with its wild goats and its walls of peculiarly striped red and white rock.

Sun-washed Geraldton, Dongara and the Greenough Plains that lie between them were centres of early settlement. Geraldton is gateway to the Abrolhos, three groups of islands with a seasonal population of crayfishermen and a more permanent one of sea birds, who breed there.

The coastal stretch north of Perth is where you find the Pinnacles and the grey-green banksia bush around Eneabba. A quiet landscape, it has many unique wildflowers.

But it is the area inland from Geraldton and stretching to Paynes Find where wildflowers are to be seen at their most spectacular. Everlastings bloom there in great sheets in the spring. Often in August or September, with family and friends I have camped near Paynes Find with its old gold workings and being there in amongst the flowers has been a constant source of delight to us. There is all the discovery and excitement of the unpredictable natural world here, away from the predictability of man-made things and places.

Coastline Peron Peninsula.

Our Lady of Carmel Church, Mullewa – work of John Hawes, a priest-architect.

Music room at the Benedict Monastery, New Norcia.

Two aspects of the Eneabba Landscape: The eroded tableland (left). Blackboy forest (above).

Above and left: At the Pinnacles, Nambung National Park.
Limestone seeping into the cavities left by a primeval forest has produced strange shapes.

The way it was – old farm between Greenough and Geraldton, famous historic farming district.

Overlooking Geraldton to the sea.

Fishermen's huts and jetties on the Abrolhos Islands, scene of activity only during the crayfishing season.

Port Gregory with the pink waters of Hutt Lagoon in the background.

133.

Mouth of the Moore River.

Beach at Kalbarri, mouth of the Murchison.

A national emblem, come to life.

*Right: Wild goats against
the layered rocks of the
Murchison Gorge.*

The everlasting wonder of everlastings – between Payne's Find and Yalgoo.

Kalbarri Gorge
near the Z-bend.

Footsteps in the mud. Monger's Lake, west of Payne's Find.

Big Lagoon, Peron Peninsula,
Shark Bay.

Cape Inscription, Dirk Hartog Island – an historical site marking Dirk Hartog's landing here in 1616.

Visitors meet the dolphins of Monkey Mia.

Stromatolites – both fossil and living forms of ancient organisms.

Seagrass patterns,
Shark Bay. Peron Peninsula
in the background.

144.

Loggerhead turtle returning to the sea, Turtle Bay, Dirk Hartog Island.

Shell Beach, Shark Bay.

Mt Augustus – unobtrusively the world's greatest monolith.

A sense of order – plantations along the Gascoyne River.

*The modern
shepherd
at work.*

Mesa country north of Thee Springs – huge habitat for sheep.

151.

Trio of bush hats.

Country races at Landor Station. Horses seem to disappear into the Never Never on the far stretch.

This has been a very important area for the state. Gold-fever brought people here in droves in the early days. Many left; some stayed. And everywhere are strewn the relics – the poppet-heads, the shafts and the mullock-heaps – all testifying to the old ways of doing things when it was individuals who laboured to wrest the precious metal from the ground. I have always been intrigued by this visible evidence of human endeavour and endurance, so well-captured by early photographers; and I feel I too want to catch them before they completely disappear.

For things have changed on the goldfields. The days of romance are over. Now it is the time of the big mining companies, and of modern methods that scoop huge holes in the ground. Yet it is this very mining technology that makes the industry still viable. Kalgoorlie's fabulous Golden Mile still yields its riches; there are workings at Norseman, Meekatharra, Wiluna and Mt. Magnet; and in between them lie the ghosts of towns like Lawler's Ruins where they just walked away when the easy gold ran out.

But gold is not the only mineral of the region. Nickel mining is an important second and has injected new life into the goldfields, as at Kambalda. And the search goes on for other minerals – uranium for one.

The early development of the goldfields was due to a significant feat of engineering. C.Y. O'Connor's achievement of building a pipeline bringing water from Perth made life tolerable, even possible, for the miners – and also for the farmers along the way. Some of the great wheat-growing areas lie between Kalgoorlie and Perth. Towns such as Toodyay, Merredin and York are still centres of agriculture, all connected by railway and by the umbilical cord of pipeline that has sustained so many for so long.

Esperance, on the coast, has opened up a relatively new area; it is a supply port and a kind of escape hatch for those weary of the dust and the dryness of the inland. It also is linked with the south-west. The sea there is littered with islands – the Recherche Archipelago, haunt of seals, and once of pirates. The Cape Le Grand National Park shows nature on the scale its name suggests. And there are strange pink lakes coloured by micro-organisms that can be seen not far from Esperance, and on Middle Island in the Recherche group.

Eucla, near the South Australian border is an interesting place. It is cradled in ever-changing sand dunes and there you can see the great cliffs of the Bight plunging into the sea.

The context of the goldfields is space. To the west lie the marginal wheat lands, to the east the emptiness of the Nullabor, a vast treeless plain. Forming a barrier to the Eastern States, it has helped to maintain the isolation in which this state has developed. To undertake a journey across it on foot, as the early explorers did must have been something on the scale of a space voyage. As I drive across it in these times I wonder at their achievement in the face of the vastness of this great land.

Mt Charlotte – modern gold-mining poppet head.

Men of the land checking one of our main export crops.

Wheat harvesting patterns,
south of Merredin.

At the end of the dry season supplementary feeding becomes necessary.

*Radial tracks run where sheep
gather to the hub of water.*

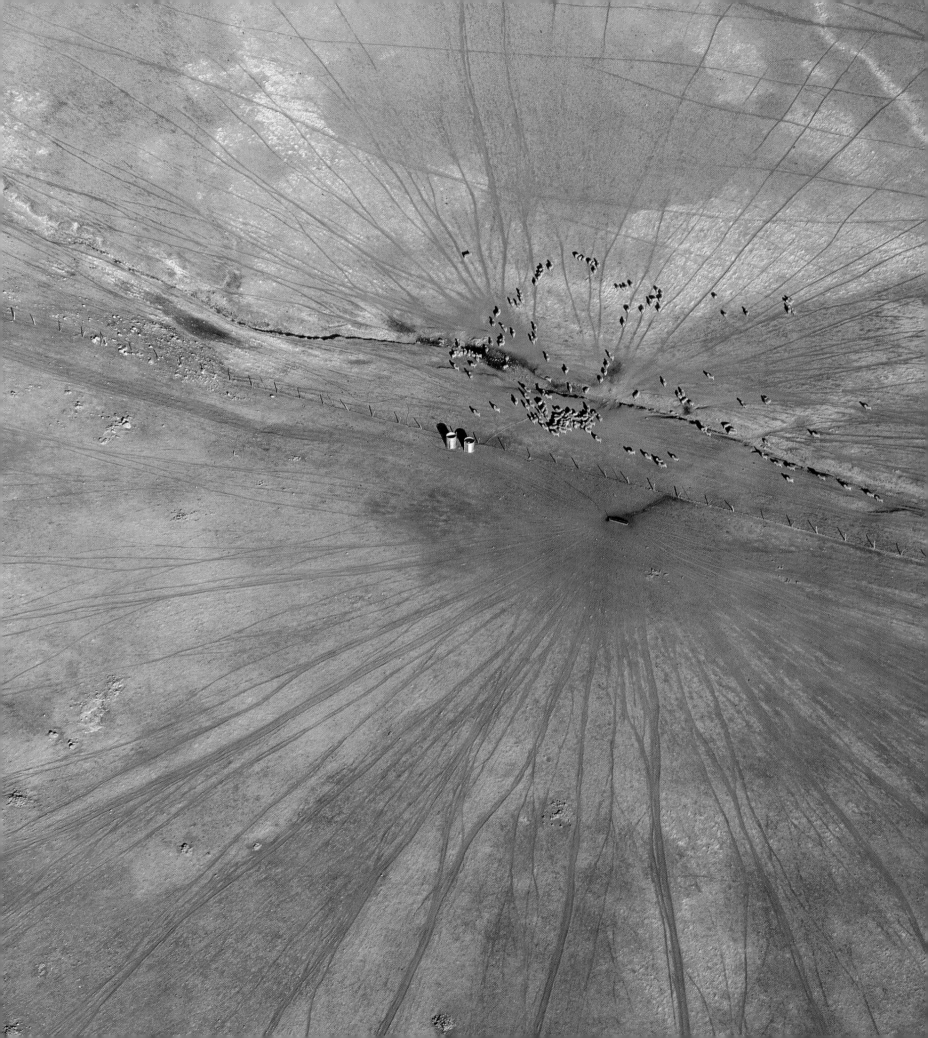

Old Northam Town Hall reflects the dignity and civic pride of the old country towns.

Northam is a venue for all kinds of aerial activity. The pipeline in the background threads its way through the wheatfields of the Avon Valley, headed for the goldfields.

Wave Rock, Hyden.

York. The first inland
farming town settled in
Western Australia.

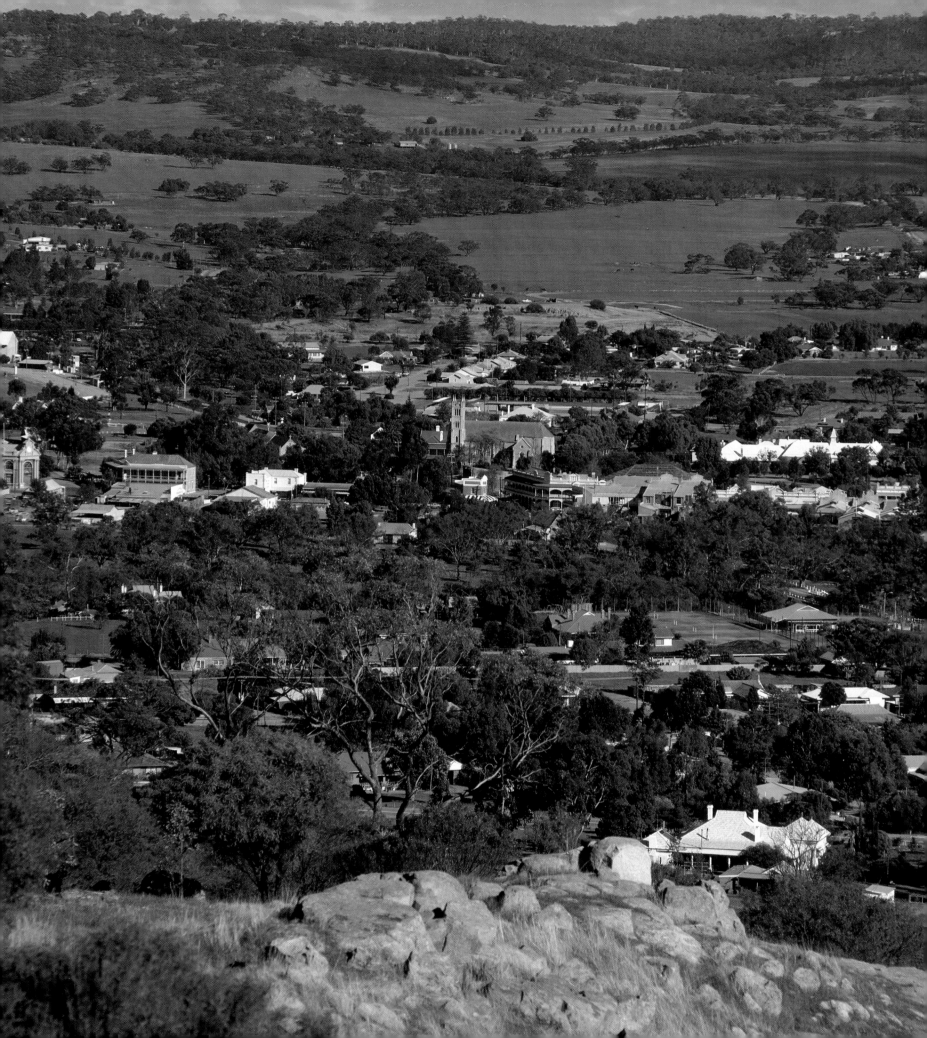

Days end – Coolgardie.

164.

Coolgardie – remembering the old days.

Old Mill and Museum, main street of Toodyay.

The Main Street, Cue.

Filigree of gimlet gums back-lit by sunset.

Bush factory. Women making aboriginal artefacts.

Old-timers, Boulder.

A two-up school in the back-blocks of Kalgoorlie.

Kalgoorlie – view down Hannan Street.

*Kalgoorlie Golden Mile is slowly disappearing into
a great hole in the ground. With it goes something of
the romance associated with mining in the early days.*

View across Hannan Street to the Exchange Hotel.

Boulder Block, one of the few old buildings not yet swallowed up by mining excavations.

The Railway Hotel and the Anzac Memorial – features of many country towns.

Back into the light – one of the few remaining underground miners.

All for this. A ton of gold, Perth Mint.

Percussion drill at work on Lake Lefroy to determine the extent of a nickel ore deposit.

Traffic in the open cut of a nickel and gold mine, Kambalda.

Surveyor using the latest in mining technology.

An increasing number of women are involved in the heavy side of the industry. Truck drivers at the Kambalda open cut mine.

Salt of the earth – camp cook.

*At an outback mustering
campfire in the west.*

*Cliffs along the coastline
edging the Nullabor Plain.*

185.

This forms the lower corner of the state from Mandurah, below Perth past Albany on the south coast as far as Esperance. It is the most intensely developed area, due to the kindliness of its predictable rainfall and to the richness of its soil. The feeling I have here is one of a nurturing environment, for the land yields an abundance of timber, wheat, wool and wine. The European might well feel more at home here than in the scoured landscapes of the north.

The coastline has always been a great inspiration to me, particularly that between Busselton and Augusta. All along this coast there is beautiful evidence of the ceaseless struggle between land and sea; it is a challenge to me to photograph; and I never tire of contemplating its wildness and its timelessness. The south coast, between Augusta and Albany is just as rugged but there is some relief from the relentless waves in the way of protected bays and inlets – Wilson's Inlet at Denmark is one – which allow undisturbed boating and fishing. Albany, situated on a magnificent natural harbour, is where the first white settlers came, and where people still come to escape Perth's summer heat.

Denmark sees the beginning of the great karri forests which sweep up in a wide arc through what is known as the Valley of the Giants. Here the landscape tends to the vertical, unlike the horizontal planes of the Pilbara and Murchison. I find it hard to do photographic justice to those trees, for being in amongst them is a three-dimensional experience, difficult to transmit on film.

Majestically the huge karri trees hold up their canopies against the light, allowing plants, animals and birds to flourish in their calm shade. Their timber is highly prized; Pemberton and Manjimup are centres of tree-felling activity. But the area has been exploited to the point of concern. There is now an increasing awareness of the value of these forests as they stand – not as they fall.

The Stirling Ranges are to me another highlight of the South West. Great picture-book mountains heave up out of a quiet plain in such a way that they present a dramatically clear image to the viewer. I have been a frequent visitor for many years, climbed every peak and revelled in the subtlety and variety of its vegetation. The Porongorups further south-west are another group of mountains, the softer, forest-clad outlines of which contrast with the Stirlings' thrust and boldness.

Further inland lies the enormous wheatbelt and the grazing areas. Wool and wheat are primary exports that provide much of the wealth of the state. But it is an area not without its problems. The government initiated move of clearing and fencing a million acres a year in the fifties, has proved disastrous for the marginal land. The denuding of bushlands has driven the underground salt to the surface, so that now most of the rivers of the south-west are brackish. Economically this region feeds and clothes us so we can feel some gratitude for its productivity. It has become a matter of striking a balance between this provision of essentials, and what the land can take. Farmers and government recognise this and are attempting to heal the land in various ways, one of them being the planting of trees.

Typical south-west scene near Denmark. Wilson's Inlet in the background.

The thriving city of Bunbury on the west coast, south of Perth.

The Vasse River at Busselton. A place to relax.

One of the many small wineries in the South West.

The verandah of Wonnerup
House, an old homestead
near Busselton.

David Gregg, pioneer of Margaret River wine making industry.

David Hohnen, winemaker, Cape Mentelle Winery, near Margaret River.

*The Leeuwin Estate Concert,
held in the winery, this annual
festival brings many people
from Perth, as well as the locals.*

Witchcliffe General Store, one of the few left in the South West.

Marybrook, a holiday resort and restaurant in a beautiful forest setting near Margaret River.

Man and best friend, fishing Blackwood River, Augusta.

Boy and best mate.

Cleaning the early morning catch at Hardy Inlet, Augusta.

Karri Valley Resort near Pemberton.

One of the caves that honeycomb the area between Yallingup and Augusta.

Hovea and wattle in the karri forest.

The Warren River shrouded in karri forest.

Canoing,
Warren
River.

Fresh water stream finding its way to the sea.

*Fishing,
William Bay.*

Fishing,
Canal Rocks.

Mustering sheep, the Stirling Range looming beyond.

The shearing team presents –

Road through karri forest near Pemberton.

Princess Harbour, Albany. Mt Many Peaks in the background.

Late afternoon light falls on Albany.

Worsley Alumina Refinery near Collie.

Working at Worsley.

Esperance – an overview.

*Old Whaling Station,
now a museum, Albany.*

Trout hatchery, south of Pemberton.

The rugged coastline south of Albany.

Rocky Point,
Cape Naturaliste.